FAUST

in Full Score

Including the Romance: "Si le bonheur,"
the unabridged "Walpurgis Night" and "Bacchanal"
and the complete "Faust Ballet Music"

CHARLES GOUNOD

DOVER PUBLICATIONS, INC.
New York

Bibliographical Note

This Dover edition, first published in 1994, is a republication in one volume of two full scores and one score excerpt originally published separately. Ed. Bote & G. Bock, Berlin, n.d., originally published the full score of the opera in a German/French edition under the title *Margarete (Faust): Oper in fünf Akten Nach Goethe von Jules Barbier und Michel Carré. Deutsche Übersetzung von J. Behr. Musik von Charles Gounod. Vollständige Orchester-Partitur Durchgesehen von F. H. Schneider.* Chappell & Co. Ltd., London, n.d., originally published *Ballet Music: Faust composed by Charles Gounod. Full Score*, consisting of the complete ballet music in seven movements. Mapleson Music Publications, New York, n.d., originally published *Romance:* "Si le bonheur" as part of the full score of the opera under the title *Faust. Grand Opera in Five Acts with French and English Text. Music by Charles Gounod.*

The Dover edition adds: expanded lists of credits and characters; a new listing of contents, with editorial notes on optional cuts and insertions and on the roles of the chorus; an instrumentation list and glossary; an appendix containing music omitted in the Bote & Bock score, with new headings in French and English; a performance note on p. 266; and English translations of four German footnotes.

Library of Congress Cataloging-in-Publication Data

Gounod, Charles, 1818–1893.
    [Faust. German & French]
    Faust : including the romance Si le bonheur, the unabridged Walpurgis night and Bacchanal, and the complete Faust ballet music / Charles Gounod.—In full score.
    1 score.
    Libretto by Jules Barbier adapted from the play by Michel Carré, based on the poem by Goethe.
    Reprint. Originally published: Berlin : Bote & Bock, n.d. (opera); London : Chappell, n.d. (ballet music); New York : Mapleson Music, n.d. (romance Si le bonheur).
    ISBN 0-486-28349-6
    1. Operas—Scores. 2. Faust, d. ca. 1540—Drama. I. Barbier, Jules, 1825–1901. II. Carré, Michel, 1819–1872. III. Goethe, Johann Wolfgang von, 1749–1832. Faust. 1. Theil. IV. Title.
M1500.G71F24   1994   94-30253
                                                                          CIP
                                                                                   M

Manufactured in the United States of America
Dover Publications, Inc., 31 East 2nd Street, Mineola, N.Y. 11501

FAUST*

Opera in Five Acts

Libretto by Jules Barbier
adapted from Michel Carré's play *Faust et Marguerite* (before 1856),
based on Johann Wolfgang von Goethe's dramatic poem *Faust, Part One* (1808)

MUSIC BY CHARLES GOUNOD

Additional Words and Music
Texts of "Chanson du Roi de Thulé" and "Chanson du Veau d'or" by Michael Carré
"Bacchanal" by Louis Schindelmeisser
Romance: "Si le bonheur" and complete "Faust Ballet Music" by Charles Gounod

First performance (as an opéra dialogué)
Théâtre-Lyrique, Paris: 19 March 1859

With recitatives replacing dialogue
Strasbourg: April 1860

With ballet
Opèra, Paris: 3 March 1869

CHARACTERS

Marguerite, *a young woman* . . . . .Soprano
Siebel, *a village boy in love with Marguerite* . . . . .Soprano
Marthe Schwerlein, *Marguerite's neighbor* . . . . .Mezzo-soprano
Faust, *an aging scholar* . . . . .Tenor
Valentin, *Marguerite's brother, a soldier* . . . . .Baritone
Brander (Wagner), *a student* . . . . .Baritone
Mephistopheles, *the Devil disguised as a gentleman* . . . . .Bass

Students, Soldiers, Villagers, Evil Spirits, Angels,
Courtesans and Queens of Antiquity

Setting: Germany in the 16th century

*Called *Margarete (Faust)* in the German version

FAUST'S CHORUSES

In addition to generic appearances in full score as "Chor" ("Ch.") or "Männerchor" ("Mch."), all or sections of *Faust*'s large vocal ensemble appear in more than a dozen roles. Each role is identified below in English, French and German, with its score abbreviation in parentheses. Page numbers mark first appearances in the work.

CHORUS OF YOUNG WOMEN (p. 15)
 [Chœur des jeunes filles / Frauenchor (Frch.)]
CHORUS OF PEASANTS (18)
 [Chœur des laboureurs / Chor der Landleute (Mch.)]
STUDENTS (58)
 [Étudiants / Studenten (St.)]
SOLDIERS (62)
 [Soldats / Soldaten (So.)]
PEOPLE OF THE TOWN (64)
 [Bourgeois, Bürger (Bg. / Ch.)]
YOUNG GIRLS (66)
 [Jeunes filles / Junge Mädchen (Jg. Md.)]
YOUNG STUDENTS (67)
 [Jeunes étudiants / Junge Studenten (Jg. St.)]
MATRONS (68)
 [Matrones / Matronen (Mt.)]
MEN'S CHORUS (86)
 [Männerchor (Mch.)]
CHORUS OF DEMONS (271)
 [Chœur de démons / Geister-Chor (Mch.)]
CHURCH CHOIR (275)
 [Chant religieux / Geistlicher Chor (Ch.)]
WILL-'O-THE-WISP CHORUS (364)
 [Chœur des feux follets / Chor der Irrlichter (Ch.)]
QUEENS AND COURTESANS OF ANTIQUITY (398)
 [Chor (Ch.)]
HEAVENLY CHOIR (455)
 [Voix d'en haut / Himmlischer Chor]
GENERAL CHORUS (457)
 [Chœur général / Allgemeiner Chor (Ch.)]

CONTENTS

ACT I / 3
Faust's study

SCENE 1
(*Faust, Chorus*)

SCENE 2

(*Mephistopheles, Faust*)

ACT II / 55

At the village gate and inn

SCENE 1

(*Chorus, Wagner*)

SCENE 2

(*Valentin, Wagner, Siebel, Chorus*)

SCENE 3

(*Mephistopheles joins the others*)

SCENE 4

(*Mephistopheles, Faust*)

SCENE 5

(*Chorus, Mephistopheles, Faust, Siebel, Marguerite*)

ACT III / 154
Marguerite's garden

SCENE 1
(Siebel)

SCENE 2
(Faust, Mephistopheles, Siebel)

SCENE 3
(Mephistopheles, Faust)

SCENE 4
(Faust)

SCENE 5
(Mephistopheles, Faust)

SCENE 6
(Marguerite)

SCENE 7
(Marthe, Marguerite)

SCENE 8
(Mephistopheles and Faust join the women)

Prenez mon bras un moment! 199 / Ainsi, vous voyagez
toujours? 201 / Eh quoi! toujours seule?—Mon frère est
soldat 204 / *Quartet:* Je ne vous crois pas!—Laisse-moi
ton bras!—Ne m'accusez pas—Vous n'entendez pas 207

SCENE 9
(Siebel, Marthe, Mephistopheles)

Du courage! Je veux tout lui dire! 213

SCENE 10
(Mephistopheles)

Il était temps!—O nuit, étends sur eux ton ombre 216

SCENE 11
(Marguerite, Faust)

Il se fait tard—Laisse-moi—O silence, ô bonheur! 221 / O nuit
d'amour 229 / Marguerite!—Ah! partez! 231

SCENE 12
(Mephistopheles, Faust)

Tête folle!—Tenez! Elle ouvre sa fenêtre 240

SCENE 13
(Marguerite, Faust, Mephistopheles)

Il m'aime! Il m'aime! 242

ACT IV / 249
Marguerite's room (Scenes 1, 2)

SCENE 1
(Marguerite, Chorus)

Elles ne sont pas là—Le galant étranger s'enfuit 252 /
[optional] "Spinning Song": Il ne revient pas! 256

SCENE 2
(Siebel, Marguerite)

Marguerite! . . . Siebel! 264 / *[optional] Romance:* Si le bonheur
[see Appendix, p. 465] . . . Soyez béni, Siebel 266

SCENE 3
In the church
(Marguerite, Mephistopheles, Chorus)

Seigneur, daignez permettre 269 / Souviens-toi du passé 272 / Quand
du Seigneur—Non! pour toi 275 / Seigneur, accueillez la prière 281

SCENE 4

The street fronting Marguerite's house and the church
(Marthe, Siebel, Valentin, Soldiers)

SCENE 5

(Valentin, Siebel)

SCENE 6

(Faust, Mephistopheles)

SCENE 7

(Valentin joins the two)

SCENE 8

(Marthe, Chorus, Valentin, Marguerite, Siebel)

ACT V / 362

SCENE 1

In the Harz Mountains
(Chorus, Mephistopheles, Faust)

SCENE 2

The Courtesans' Palace

*According to German superstition, a witches' Sabbath took place on the Brocken, a peak of the Harz Mountains, on
the eve of May Day during the feast of the saint Walpurga. A note about the various performance options affecting
Faust's "Walpurgis Night" appears on page v.

APPENDIX / 463

INSTRUMENTATION

2 Flutes (Flute 2 doubles Piccolo) [Flöten, Fl., gr. Fl. (2te kleine Flöte, kl. Fl.)]
2 Oboes (Oboe 2 doubles English Horn) [Oboen, Ob. (Englisch Horn, Engl. Hr.)]
2 Clarinets in A, B♭ [Klarinetten, Klar. (A, B)]
2 Bassoons [Fagotte, Fag.]

4 Horns in C, D♭, D, E♭, E, F, A, B♭-basso [Hörner, Hör., Hr. (C, Des, D, Es, E,
     F, A, tief B)]

{ 2 Trumpets in C, D, E♭, B♭ [Trompeten, Trp. (C, D, Es, B)]
     doubling
{ 2 Cornets in A,.B♭ [Kornetts, Korn. (A, B)]
3 Trombones [Posaunen, Pos.]

Timpani [Pauken, Pk.]
Percussion:
     Snare Drum [kleine Trommel, kl. Trm.]
     Bass Drum and Cymbals [Grosse Trommel, gr. Trm(l). u(nd) Becken, Beck.]
     Triangle [Triangel, Trgl.]
     Tam-Tam [Tamtam, Tamt.]

4 Harps [Harfe(n), Hrf.]
Organ [Orgel, Org.]

Violins 1, 2 [Violinen, Viol.]
Violas [Bratschen, Br.]
Cellos [Violoncelle, Vcll.]
Basses [Kontrabässe, Kbss.]

Optional Stage Band (Act. IV, Sc. 4)
[Bühnenmusik nach Belieben]:
     Soprano Saxophone in E♭ [Sopran-Saxhorn, Sopr.-Sxh. (Es)]
     2 Cornets in B♭ [Kornetts, Korn. (B)]
     2 Trumpets in E♭ [Trompeten, Trp. (Es)]
     2 Alto Trombones in E♭ [Altposaunen, Altpos. (Es)]
     Tenor Trombone in C [Tenorposaune, Tenpos. (C)]
     Bass Saxophone in B♭ [Bass-Saxhorn, Bass-Sxh. (B)]
     Contrabass Saxophone in B♭ [Kontrabässe-Saxhorn, Kbss.-Sxh. (B)]

Note: For his "Serenade" (Act IV, Sc. 6), Mephistopheles "plays" a prop guitar.

A GLOSSARY OF GERMAN PERFORMANCE WORDS IN THE ORCHESTRAL SCORE

alle, all (*tutti*)
As, A-flat
auch, also, too

B, B-flat
beim Sprung, optional cut

Des, D-flat
die übr(igen), the others

ein(e), one
Es, E-flat
etwas langsamer als, somewhat slower than

gedämpft, damped [for a drum]
get(eilt), divided (*divisi*)

H, B-natural
hinter der Szene, off-stage

mit Dämpfer, muted (*con sordino*)
mit dem, with the

natürl(ich), naturally, in the usual way
nicht get(eilt), non-divisi
nimmt, change to [a different instrument]

ohne Dämpfer, without mute (*senza sordino*)

Rezit(ation), recitative

später, later

umstimmen (*e in es*, etc.), tune to another pitch (E to E♭, etc.)
u(nd), and

von, from, by, of

Zeitmasse, tempo
zu 2, both instruments (*a2*)
zus(ammen), together, unison

MARGARETE
(FAUST)
Oper in fünf Akten
von
CH. GOUNOD

Akt I	Acte I
Nr. 1 Introduktion	Nº 1 Introduction

1. Szene

Faust allein

Fausts Studierzimmer

Nr. 2 Szene und Chor

Scène I

Faust, seul

Le cabinet de Faust

N⁰ 2 Scène et Chœur

(Der Morgen beginnt zu grauen. Faust öffnet das Fenster.)
(Le jour commence à poindre. Faust va ouvrir sa croisée.)

(Er nimmt ein Fläschchen vom Tische.)

Faust: Wohl - an, mit dir, o Tod, vereint mich dieser La - be-trank!
Eh bien! puis-que la mort me fuit, Pourquoi n'al-lé-je pas vers el-le?

(Il saisit une fiole sur la table)

Andante maestoso

Faust: O Tag, dir gilt mein letzter Gruß, o
Sa - lut! ô mon dernier ma - tin! Sa-

ins — Stübchen lacht, — Vög - lein im bunten Kleid sin - get sein Lied, — Licht - strahl an Lichtstrahl reiht, Dämmrung ent-
Sous son manteau d'or; — De - jà l'oi - seau chan - te Ses fol - les chan-sons; — L'aube ca - res-san - te Sou-rit aux mois-

flieht, — sil — ber - ne Quel - le fließt auf grü - ner Flur, — Blu - me der Knosp' entsprießt und Lieb' der Na - tur, —
sons; — Le ruis-seau mur-mu - re, La fleur s'ouvre au jour, — Tou-te la na - tu - re S'é-veille à — l'a - mour!

Nr. 3 Rezitativ — № 3 Récitatif

Faust:
Macht, der See - le Trieb, verflucht sei Glück, sei Ruhm und Macht! Der Hoff - nung Fluch und Fluch der Lieb'. Fluch dir, Ge-
poir qui passe a - vec l'heu - re, Rê - ves d'a - mour ou de com - bats! Maudit soit le bon - heur, maudi - tes la sci - en - ce,

duld, Fluch dir, Ge-duld! Sa-tan, her-bei! Sa-tan, her - bei! Her-bei zu mir!____ Sa-tan, her-bei!____

La prière et la foi! Maudi-te sois-tu,____ pa-ti-en-ce! A moi, Sa-tan!____ à moi!

2. Szene
Faust und Mephistopheles
Nr. 4 Duett

Scène II
Faust et Méphistophélès
Nº 4 Duo

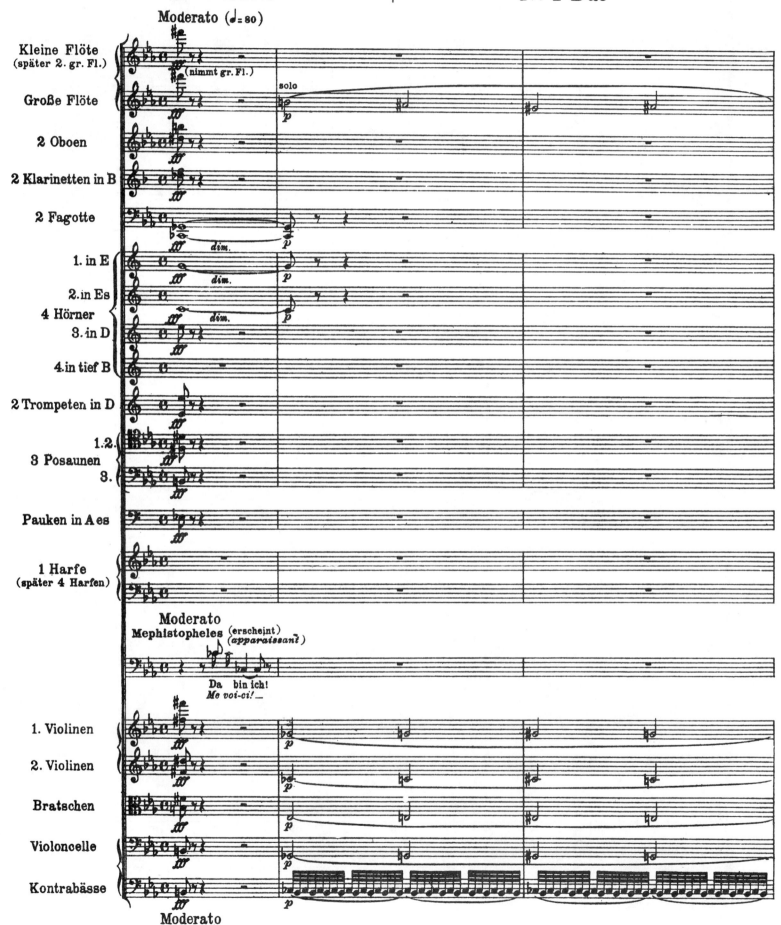

Allegro ben marcato (♩=100)

Fl.

Ob.

Klar.B

Fag.

1.E
2.Es
Hör.
3.D
4.tief B

1.2.
Pos.
3.

Pk.

Hrf.

(Faust leert die Schale und verwandelt sich in einen
eleganten Junker. Die Erscheinung verschwindet.)

(Faust vide la coupe et se trouve métamorphosé en
jeune et élégant seigneur.—La vision disparaît.)

Allegro ben marcato
Mephistopheles

Komm!
Viens!—

1.Viol.

2.Viol.

Br.

Vcll.

Kbss.

Allegro ben marcato

Faust:
Glück,____ ich fühl'____ neu-en Mut,____ und Kraft____ kehrt zu - rück!____ Ich fühl'____ sü - ße
tres - - ses! A moi ____ leurs ca - res - - ses, A moi____ leurs dé - sirs! ____ A moi ____ l'é-ner-

Meph:
win - - ket der Mägd -lein Kuß, ____ und wonni-ger Trieb ____ ver-eint uns zur Lust; ____ warm
jeu - - nes maî-tres - - ses! ____ A toi leurs ca - res - - ses, A toi leurs dé - sirs! ____ A

48

Ende des 1sten Aktes
Fin du 1er Acte

Akt II

Vor einem Stadttor. Zur Linken eine Herberge mit dem Schilde: „Zum Gott Bacchus"

1. Szene

Brander, junge Mädchen, Matronen,
Bürger, Studenten, Soldaten

Nr. 5 Allgemeiner Chor (Kirmeß)

Acte II

Une des portes de la ville. A gauche, un cabaret à l'enseigne du dieu Bacchus

Scène I

Wagner, jeunes filles, matrones, bourgeois
étudiants, soldats

N° 5 Choeur (Une kermesse)

Nas-se trinkt er gern, bleibt das Was-ser ihm fern, und ihm win-ken Ruhm und Lieb', wo zu trin-ken es
dep-te Du ton-neau, N'en ex-cep-te Que l'eau! Que ta gloi-re, Tes a-mours Soient de boi-re Tou-

denn solch wil - den Gä-sten ist das leich - tes Spiel! Wer es kühn un - ter-nom-men als ein
Vieux bourgs, jeu - nes maî-tresses Sont pour nous un jeu! Ce - lui qui sait__ s'y pren-dre Sans trop

tapf-rer Held, wird sie si - cher__ be-kom-men und das Lö-se-geld, ja, das Lö-se-geld!__
de__ fa-çon, Les o-bli-ge à__ se__ ren-dre En pa-yant ran-çon, en pay-ant ran-çon!__

Bürger
Bourgeois

1ter Tenor

Sonntags und an Fei - er - ta - gen, da plaudr'ich gern von Krieg und Streit, wäh-rend sich die
Aux jours de di - manche et de fê - te, J'ai-me à par-ler guerre et combats: Tan-dis que les

Völ - ker weit, ih - re Köpfe zer-schla - gen. Um Län - der kämpft der Türk und Ruß, ich a-ber sitz im weichen Gra - se
peup-les là-bas Se cassent la _ tê - te, Je vais m'asseoir sur les coteaux Qui sont voisins de la ri - viè - re,

auf dem Hü-gel dort am Fluß, trink aus vol-lem Gla - se! Um Län-der kämpft der Türk und Ruß, ich a-ber sitz im weichen
Et je vois pas - ser les bateaux En vi-dant mon ver - re! Je vais m'asseoir sur les coteaux Qui sont voisins de la ri-

2. Szene

Valentin, Brander, Siebel, Studenten-Chor

Nr. 6 Szene und Rezitativ

Scène II

Valentin, Wagner, Siebel, étudiants

№ 6 Scène et Récitatif

Valentin (tritt auf, eine silberne Medaille in der Hand)
(paraissant, il tient une petite médaille d'argent à la main)

O hei - liges Sinn - bild, das meinGretchen mir gab, den Tod_ stets ab-zu-

O sain-te mé-dail - le Qui me viens de ma sœur, Au jour_ de la ba-

(Hängt die Medaille um den Hals und geht nach der Schenke zu.)
(Il passe la médaille à son cou et se dirige vers le cabaret.)

Valentins Gebet
Einlage von Gounod

Invocation
Supplément de Gounod

*) Falls Valentins Gebet nicht gesungen wird, Sprung zum gleichen Zeichen auf S. 91.

If Valentin's Invocation is omitted, cut to p. 91 as marked.

'ne Ratt', furchtsam gar und fei - ge,
Un rat plus pol - tron que bra - ve,

Brander

die sich stets ver - kroch, die saß, zeh - rend je - de Nei - ge, in dem Kel - ler - loch! 'ne
Et plus laid que beau, Lo - geait au fond d'u - ne ca - ve Sous un vieux ton - neau.... Un

3. Szene
Die Vorigen, Mephistopheles

Scene III
Les Mêmes, Méphistophélès

Nr. 7 Rondo vom goldenen Kalb | Nr. 7 Ronde du Veau d'or

Nr. 8 Schwerter-Szene und Choral | № 8 Récitatif et Choral des Épées

114

4. Szene
Mephistopheles, Faust

Scène IV
Méphistophélès, Faust

5. Szene

Die Vorigen. Junge Mädchen, Matronen,
Studenten, Bürger. Dann Siebel und Margarete.

Nr. 9 Walzer und Chor

Scène V

Les Mêmes. Jeunes filles, matrones,
étudiants, bourgeois. Puis Siebel et Marguerite.

Nº 9 Valse et Chœur

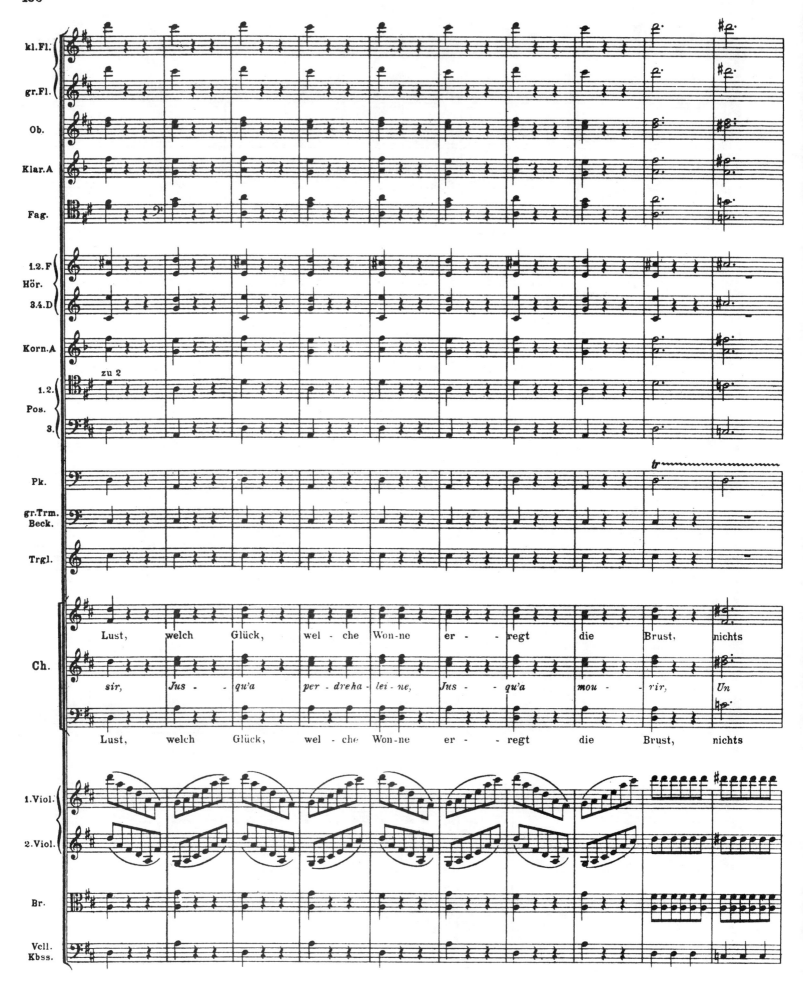

Ende des 2ten Aktes
Fin du 2me Acte

Akt III

Garten bei Margarete. Im Hintergrund eine Mauer mit Pforte. Links ein Boskett. Rechts ein Pavillon, dessen Fenster dem Publikum gegenüber liegen. Bäume und Strauchwerk.

Acte III

Le jardin de Marguerite. Au fond, un mur percé d'une petite porte. A gauche, un bosquet. A droite, un pavillon dont la fenêtre fait face au public. Arbres et massifs.

Nr. 10 Intermezzo und Lied

N°. 10 Entr'acte et couplets

1. Szene
Siebel allein

(Vorhang)
(Rideau)

Scène I
Siebel, seul

(Siebel kommt durch die Pforte und bleibt beim Pavillon neben einem Rosen- und Flieder-
busch stehen.)
(Siebel entre par la petite porte du fond et s'arrête sur le seuil du pavillon, près d'un
massif de roses et de lilas.)

2. Szene
Faust, Mephistopheles, Siebel
Nr. 11 Szene und Rezitativ

Scène II
Faust, Méphistophélès, Siebel
Nº 11 Scène et Récitatif

164

4. Szene
Faust allein
Nr. 12 Kavatine

Scène IV
Faust, seul
№ 12 Cavatine

5. Szene
Mephistopheles, Faust
Nr. 13 Szene

Scène V
Méphistophélès, Faust
№ 13 Scène

Nr. 14ª Lied vom König von Thule — Nº 14ª Chanson du Roi de Thulé

180

(Öffnet das Kästchen und läßt den Strauß fallen.)
(Elle ouvre la cassette et laisse tomber le bouquet.)

öffnen? Ha, ich be - be! Warum? Tu - e ich deshalb doch keine Sünde! O Gott! Welch reicher Schmuck! Ist's ein liebli - cher
vrais!... ma main tremble! Pourquoi? Je ne fais, en louvrant, rien de mal, je sup-pose! O Dieu! que de bi - joux! est-ce un rê-ve char-

Allegro non troppo

Traum, der mich täuscht, der mich be - lü - get und der mit sei - nem wunder-ba-ren Glanz mich be - trü - get?
mant Qui m'é-blou-it, ou si je veil-le? Mes yeux n'ont ja-mais vu de ri-ches-se pa-reil-le!

Allegro non troppo

Nr. 14ᵇ Juwelen-Arie — № 14ᵇ Air des bijoux

7. Szene
Marthe, Margarete
Nr. 15 Szene

Scène VII
Marthe, Marguerite
№ 15 Scène

Nr. 16 Quartett — № 16 Quatuor

9. Szene
Siebel, Marthe, Mephistopheles
Nr. 17 Szene

Scène IX
Siebel, Marthe, Méphistophélès
Nº 17 Scène

10. Szene

Mephistopheles allein

Scène X

Méphistophélès, seul

11. Szene
Margarete, Faust
Nr.18 Duett

Scène XI
Marguerite, Faust
№ 18 Duo

col canto
Fl.
Engl. Hr.
Klar. B
Fag.
1. 2. Hr. F
Marg.
ich fühl' es lieb-be-wußt, sei-ne Wor-te mich— be-we-gen, ich fühl' es lieb-be-
J'é-cou-te et je com-prends cet-te voix so-li-tai-re Qui chan-te, qui chan-te dans mon
1. Viol.
2. Viol.
Br.
Vcll.
col canto
poco più mosso
Engl. Hr.
Fag.
1. 2. Hr. F
(Bückt sich und pflückt eine Sternblume.)
(Elle se penche et cueille une marguerite.)
Marg.
wußt! — Laßt einmal sehn, er-lau-bet! Ein ein-fach Spiel! O
cœur! — Lais-sez un peu, de grâ-ce! Un simp-le jeu. Lais-
Faust
Was soll das?
Qu'est-ce donc?
1. Viol.
2. Viol.
Br.
Vcll.
Kbss.
poco più mosso

Adagio
Fl.
Ob.
Engl. Hr.
Klar. B
Fag.
1.2. F
Hör.
3.4. Des
Trp. C
Pk.
Hrf.
Faust
En- de!
nel- le!
1. Viol.
2. Viol.
Br.
Vcll.
Kbss.
dim.
Adagio
Adagio

12. Szene
Mephistopheles, Faust

Scène XII
Méphistophélès, Faust

13. Szene
Die Vorigen, Margarete

Scène XIII
Les Mêmes, Marguerite

Ze-phyr, es schlägt die Nachtigall, der Mondnacht Stimmen flü-stern all,— sie sagen im tau-sendstimmigen Chor: Er
chan-te, le vent mur-mu-re! Toutes les voix de la na-tu-re Me re-disent en chœur:— Il

Ende des 8ten Aktes
Fin du 3me acte

Akt IV
Margaretens Zimmer

1. Szene
Margarete allein

Nr. 19 Margarete am Spinnrad

Acte IV
La chambre de Marguerite

Scène I
Marguerite, seule

№ 19 Marguerite au Rouet

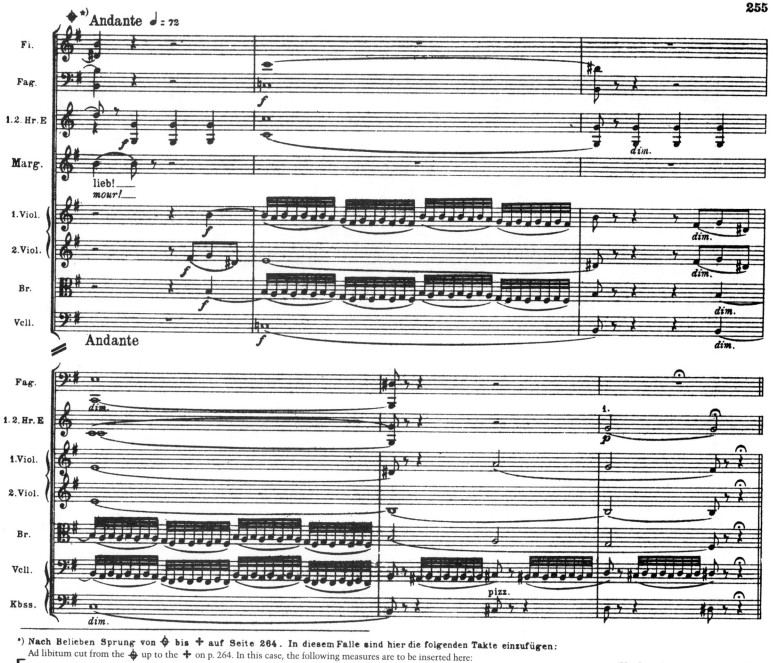

*) Nach Belieben Sprung von ✛ bis ✚ auf Seite 264. In diesem Falle sind hier die folgenden Takte einzufügen:
Ad libitum cut from the ✛ up to the ✚ on p. 264. In this case, the following measures are to be inserted here:

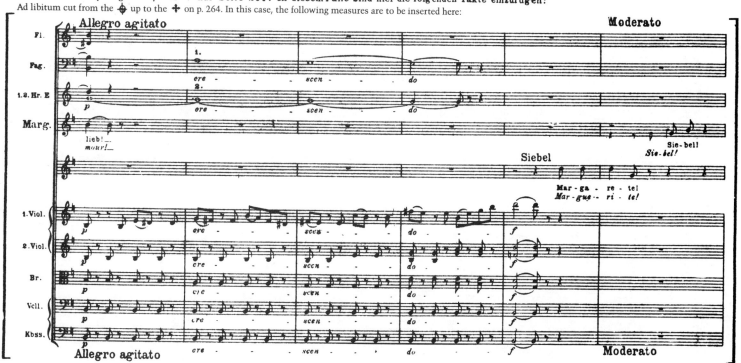

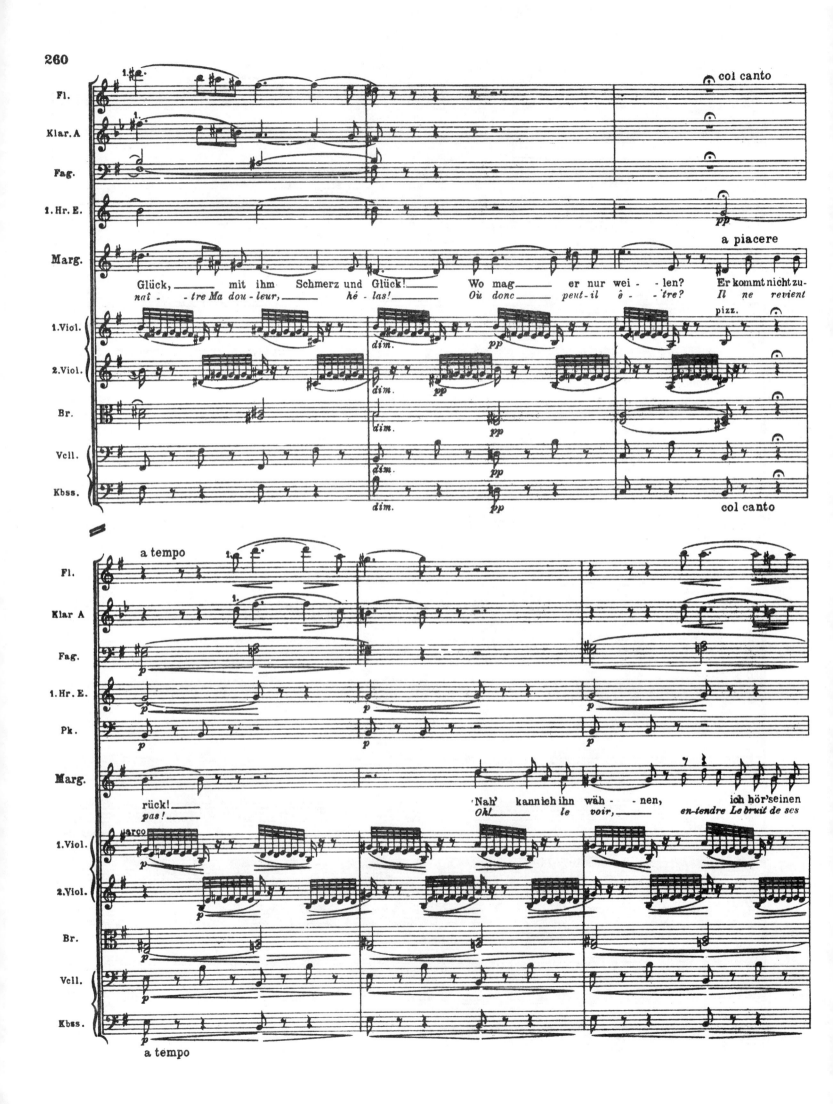

2. Szene
Siebel, Margarete
Nr. 20 Szene und Rezitativ

Scène II
Siebel, Marguerite
Nº 20 Scène et Récitatif

[Romance: "Si le bonheur" / optional insertion between Marguerite's recitative and "Soyez, béni": see Appendix, p. 465]

raubt, ich ei-le zu der Kir-che heil'gen Mauern hin, den Him-mel an-zu-flehn für mein Kind und ihn! (ab)
pas fer-mé pour moi les por-tes du Saint-lieu! J'y vais, pour mon en-fant et pour lui pri-er Dieu!(sort)

Vorhang
Rideau

Verwandlung
Changement de scène

3. Szene
Verwandlung: In der Kirche
Margarete, Mephistopheles, Chor
Nr. 21 Szene in der Kirche

Scène III
Changement de scène: l'église
Marguerite, Méphistophélès, Chœur
N° 21 Scène de l'Eglise

mehr,_____ die Welt für dich ist hoffnungs - leer,_____ hoff - - nungs - leer!_____
don, _____ *Pour toi le ciel n'a plus d'au - ro - re,* non!_____ non!_____

bei —— der Nächte Lust, —— der Liebe Schwel - ge - rei! —— Fluch dir! Fluch dir ——
dieu —— les nuits d'a - mour —— et les jours pleins d'i - vres - se! A toi mal - heur! ——

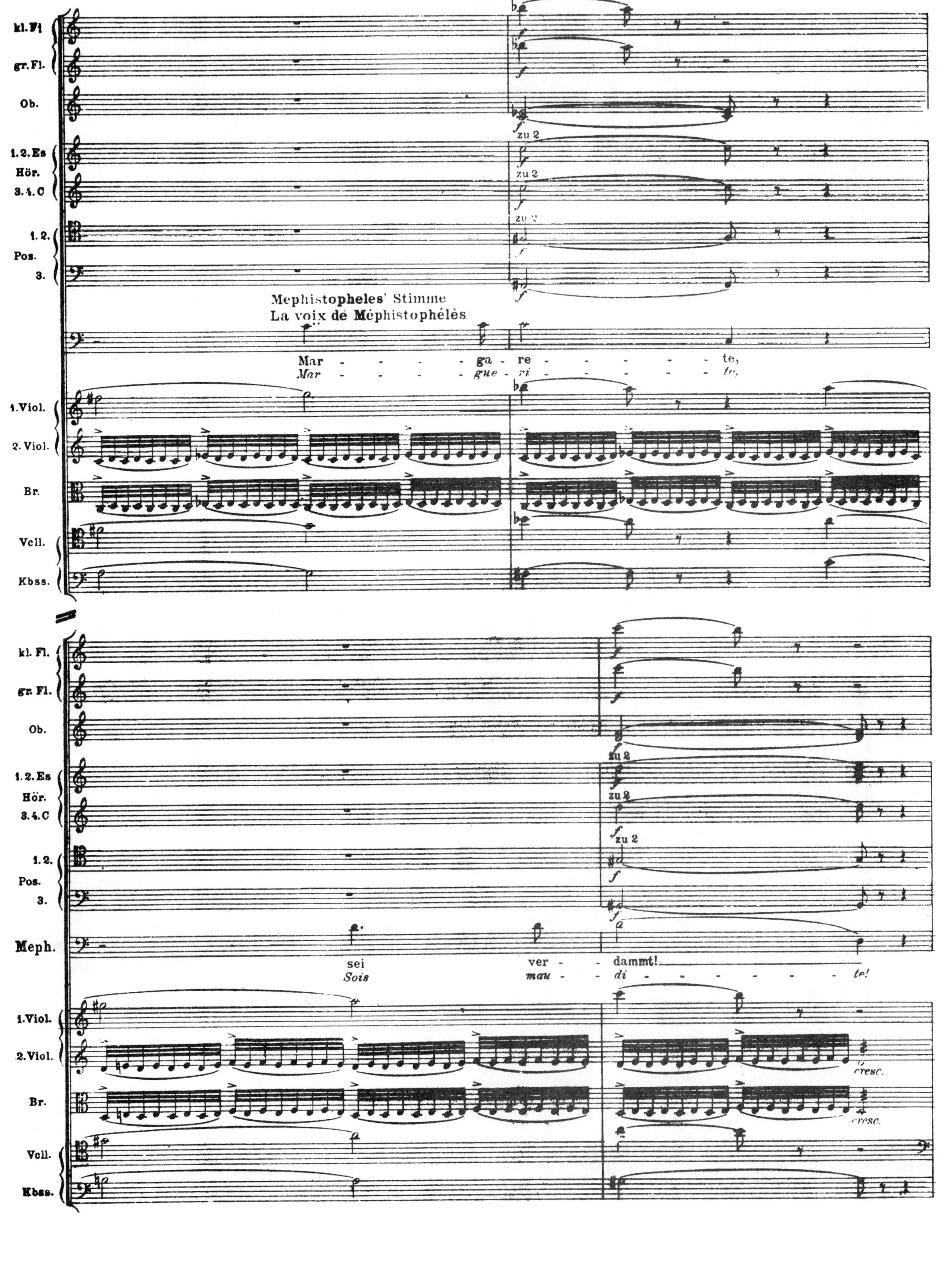
kl. Fl.
gr. Fl.
Ob.
1. 2. Es
Hör.
3. 4. C
1. 2.
Pos.
3.
zu 2
Mephistopheles' Stimme
La voix de Méphistophélès
Mar - - - - ga - re - - - - - - te,
Mar - - - - gue - ri - - - - - - te,
1. Viol.
2. Viol.
Br.
Vcll.
Kbss.
Meph.
sei ver - dammt!
Sois mau - di - - - - - - - te!
cresc.

Verwandlung
Changement de scène

4. Szene

Verwandlung: Straße; rechts Margaretens Haus, links eine Kirche

Marthe, Siebel. Dann Valentin und Soldaten.

Nr. 22 Soldatenchor

Scène IV

Changement de scène: La rue. A droite, la maison de Marguerite, à gauche, une église.

Marthe, Siebel. Puis Valentin et Soldats.

Nº 22 Chœur des Soldats

Hört Ihr sie? Ja, sie sind's! Kommt jetzt mit! O Siebel, rettet sie, o wendet ihr Geschick!
E - cou-tez! les voi-ci! Ve - nez vi-te! Sauvez la, Siebel, j'espè-re en vous!

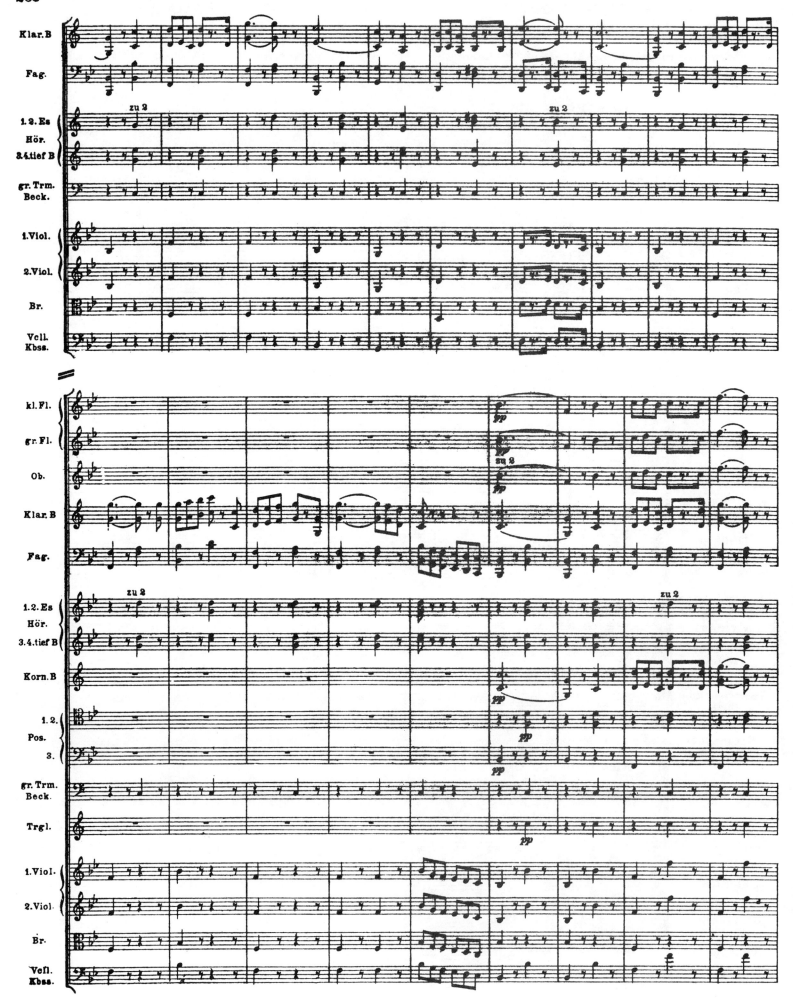

5. Szene
Valentin, Siebel
Nr. 23 Rezitativ

Scène V
Valentin, Siebel
Nº 23 Récitatif

6. Szene

Faust, Mephistopheles (eine Gitarre unterm Mantel)

Scène VI

Faust, Méphistophélès (une guitare sous son manteau)

Mephistopheles

Nun, nicht länger zögert hier, schnell tre - ten wir hin - ein!
Qu'at - tendez-vous en - co - re? en - trons dans la mai - son!

Faust

Ver-ruch-ter, schweig!
Tais-toi, mau - dit!

Nr. 24 Serenade | N° 24 Sérénade

(Er singt und begleitet sich mit der Gitarre.)
(Écartant son manteau et s'accompagnant de sa guitare)

Scheinst zu schla-fen, du im
Vous qui fai - tes l'en-dor-

7. Szene
Die Vorigen, Valentin
Nr. 25 Duell - Terzett

Scène VII
Les Mêmes, Valentin
Nº 25 Trio du Duel

Fl.
Ob.
Klar. B
Fag.
1. 2. Es
Hör.
3. 4. C
Trp. Es
1. 2.
Pos.
3.
zu 2
ff
Valentin
Wohl-an denn!
En gar - de!
Ver-teid'ge dich!
et dé-fends-toi!
Mephistopheles (zu Faust)
(à Faust)
Schließt Euch eng jetzt an mich!
Ser - rez-vous con-tre moi!
Und dann stoßet nur
Et pous-sez seu-le-
pp
1. Viol.
2. Viol.
Br.
Vcll.
Kbss.
p
(Valentin kreuzt den Degen.)
(Valentin croise le fer)
Meph.
zu! Kei-ne Sorg'! Ich pa-rie - re!
ment, chèr Docteur! moi, je pa - re!
Iter Gang
1re botte
IIter Gang
2de botte
fp

8. Szene
Marthe, Valentin, Volk mit Fackeln.
Später Margarete und Siebel.

Nr. 26 Tod Valentins

Scène VIII
Marthe, Valentin, Bourgeois.
Puis Marguerite et Siebel.

№ 26 Mort de Valentin

wa - - gen, _____ die blan - ke güld' - - - ne Ket - - te und Spit - zen -
bien en - cor, _____ O ses - tu, _____ mi - sé - ra - - ble, Gar -

flucht, bis dich er-löst___ der To-des-schlaf! Ich, ich ster-be durch dich, doch als Sol-dat___ und
di - te! La mort t'at-tend___ sur ton___gra-bat! Moi, je meurs de ta main, et je tombe en sol-

Ende des 4ten Aktes
Fin du 4e Acte

Akt V
1. Szene
Im Harzgebirge

Nr. 27 Die Walpurgisnacht

Acte V
Scène I
Les montagnes du Hartz

Nº 27 La nuit de Walpurgis

Chor der Irrlichter
Chœur des Feux follets

He-xen zum Brok-ken in Scha-ren ziehn, gelb sind die Stoppeln, die
Dans les bru - yè - res, *Dans les ro-seaux,* *Par-mi les pier - res*

Saa-ten grün, breit sind die We-ge, Vol-kes vol-lauf, wim-melnd am Ste-ge wälzt sich der Hauf.
Et sur les eaux, *De place en pla-ce,* *Per-çant la nuit,* *S'al-lume et pas-se* *Un feu qui luit!*

Ho-ho, ho-ho! Von nah und fern her-bei ihr al - le! Wir sehn euch gern,
A-ler-te, a-ler-te! *De loin, de près,* *Dans l'her-be ver-te,* *Sous le cy-près,*

(Mephistopheles und Faust erscheinen auf einem Berggipfel.)
(Méphistophélès et Faust paraissent sur une cime élevée.)

Bei Aufführung auf den deutschen Bühnen wird hier gewöhnlich das Bacchanal (Ballett) von Schindelmeißer eingelegt, das hier folgt.

In performances in German opera houses Schindelmeisser's "Bacchanal" ballet music, which follows, is usually interpolated at this point.

Einlage: Bacchanal (Ballett)

von L. Schindelmeißer

380

2. Szene

(Auf Mephistopheles' Wink öffnen sich die Berge; man sieht einen prachtvollen Palast, Königinnen und Frauen der Vorzeit beim Mahle.)

Scène II

(La montagne s'entr'ouvre et laisse voir un vaste palais resplendissant d'or, au milieu duquel se dresse une table richement servie et entourée des reines et des courtisanes de l'antiquité.)

Nr. 28 Szene und Chor
№ 28 Scène et Chœur

Fl.

Ob.

Klar. B

Fag.

1.2.F
Hör.
3.4.C

Trgl.

Hrf.

Meph.

(reicht Faust eine Schale)
(offrant une coupe à Faust)

Nimm froh die Scha - le, und magst du wähnen, Ver - ges - sen drin enthal - ten sei! ____
Prends cet - te cou - pe et que ta lè - vre Y puise l'ou - bli ____ du pas - sé! ____

Chor
Sopran

Auf, den
Que les

1.Viol.

2.Viol.

Br.

Vcll.

Kbss.

*) Wird das Bacchanal von Schindelmeißer nicht eingelegt, so kann hier die große von Gounod nachkomponierte Ballettmusik eingefügt werden, die in Partitur und Stimmen bei Ed. Bote & G. Bock, Berlin, erschienen ist. In diesem Falle geht es nach dem Ballett weiter beim Zeichen ✛ auf Seite 413.

If Schindelmeisser's "Bacchanal" is not interpolated, the extensive ballet, later composed by Gounod and published in score and parts by Bote & Bock, Berlin, can be performed at this point. In this case, after the ballet the continuation is from the sign ✛ on p. 413.

Nr. 29 Trinklied

№ 29 Chant bachique

3. Szene
Teilweise Verwandlung: Brockental

Scène III
Changement partiel: La vallée du Brocken

Ende der Walpurgisnacht
Fin de la nuit de Walpurgis

4. Szene

Verwandlung: Im Gefängnis
Margarete schlafend, Faust, Mephistopheles

Nr. 30 Gefängnis-Szene

Scène IV

Changement de scène: La prison
Marguerite, endormie, Faust, Méphistophélès

Nº 30 Scène de la Prison

a tempo
Fl.
Ob.
Klar. A
a piacere
Fag.
1. E
Hör.
3. 4. D
1. 2.
Pos.
3.
colla parte
(Der Vorhang geht auf.)
(Rideau)
1. Viol.
2. Viol.
Br.
Vcll.
Kbss.
colla parte
a tempo
zu 2
dim.
3. 4. Hr. D
Pk.
pizz.
arco

5. Szene
Faust, Margarete

Scène V
Faust, Marguerite

6. Szene
Die Vorigen, Mephistopheles
Nr. 31 Terzett-Finale

Scène VI
Les Mêmes, Méphistophélès
№ 31 Trio-Finale

444

Fl.
Klar. A
Fag.
1.2. E
Hör.
3.4. C
zu 2
Korn. A
1.2.
Pos.
3.
gr. Trm.
Beck.
Hrf.
Marg.
Schar, mei - ne See - le gnä - dig be - wahr! O
eux, Por-tez mon âme au sein des cieux! Dieu
Faust
mir, es leuch-tet schon der Mor - gen klar!
lieux, Dé - jà le jour en - va-hit les cieux!
Meph.
der Mor - gen sich, schon naht der Mor - gen, der Mor - gen klar!
de quit - ter ces lieux, Dé - jà le jour en - va-hit les cieux!
1. Viol.
2. Viol.
Br.
Vcll.
Kbss.

Nr. 32 Apotheose — № 32 Apotheose

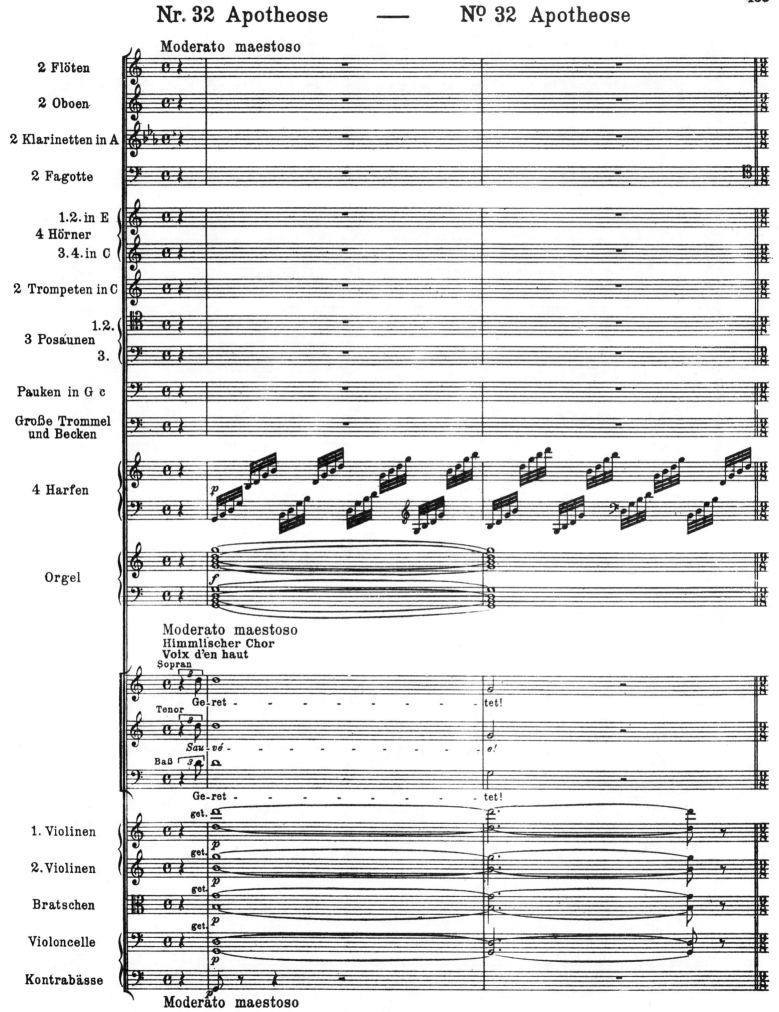

(Man hört das Glockengeläute des Ostermorgens. Die Mauern öffnen sich, und man sieht Margarete von Engeln getragen aufwärts schweben
Faust sinkt nieder, Mephistopheles stürzt unter dem Schwert des Erzengels nieder.)
(Sons de cloches de Pâques. Les murs de la prison se sont ouverts. L'âme de Marguerite s'élève dans les cieux. Faust tombe à
genoux et prie. Méphistophélès est à demi renversé sous l'épée lumineuse de l'archange.)

APPENDIX

Romance: "Si le bonheur"

bongh is left a leaf of gold, on the bough is left a leaf of gold, on the bough is left a leaf of gold.
soeur je t'ai-me-rai tou - jours, Je t'ai - me - rai tou -jours, Je t'ai - me - rai tou - jours!

Moderato.

Change in B♭

MARGARITA.

(Taking Siebel's hand)

May Heav'n re - ward thee, For all thine aid to me,.... Those who by right of
So - yez bé - ni, Sie-bel; votre a - mi - tié m'est douce! Ceux dont la main cru -

Moderato.

"Faust Ballet Music"

1. Les Nubiennes

[*Dance of the Nubian Slaves*]

2. Adagio
[*Slow Dance*]

3. Danse Antique
[*Ancient Dance*]

498

4. Variations de Cléopâtre
[*Cleopatra's Variations*]

5. Les Troyens
[Dance of the Trojan Women]

6. Variations du Miroir
[Mirror Variations]

7. Danse de Phryné
[Phryne's Dance]

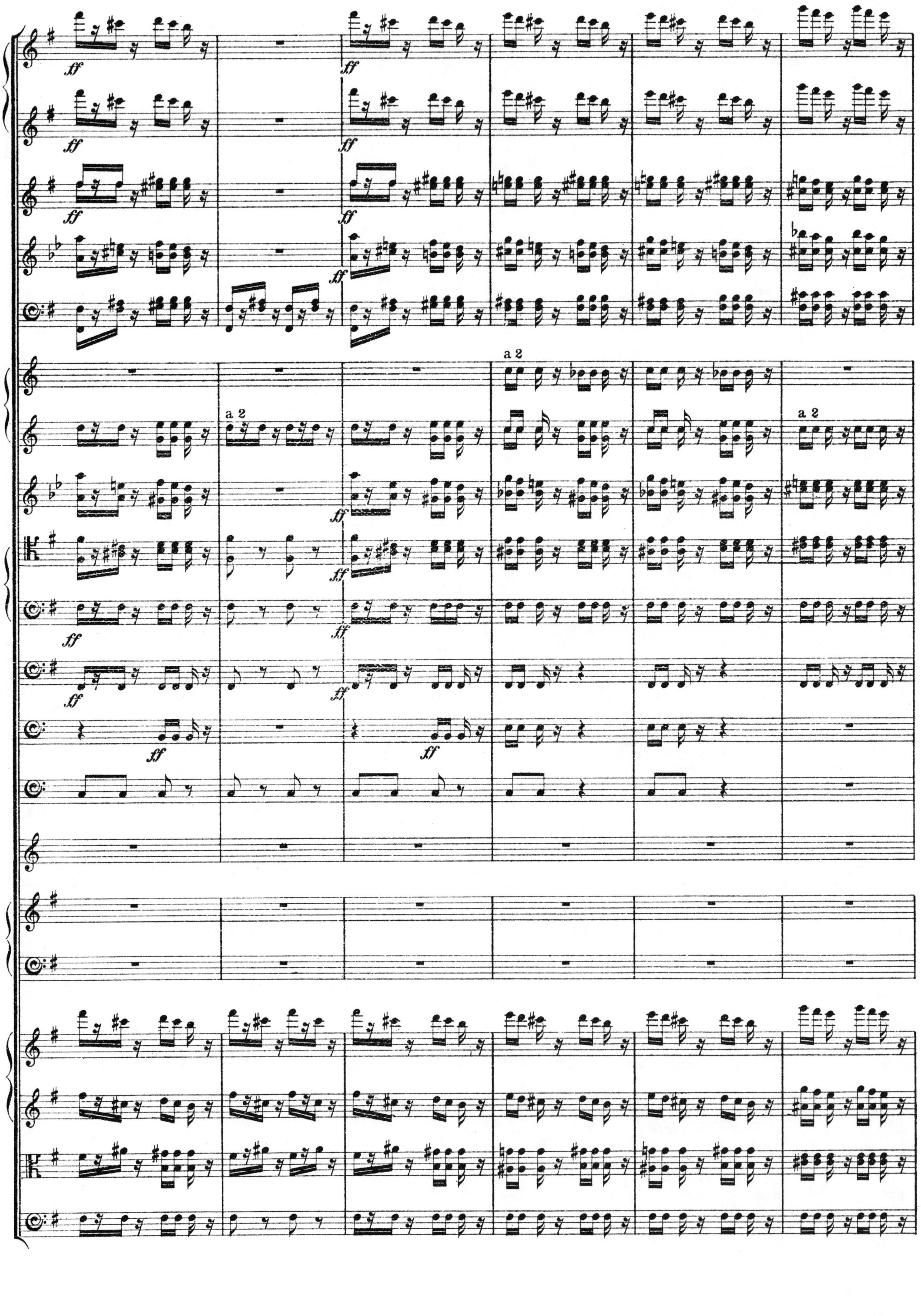
ff
a 2
a 2
a 2

Poco animato.

Poco animato.

END OF EDITION